ABLE
TO
DREAM AGAIN

KEITH LOY

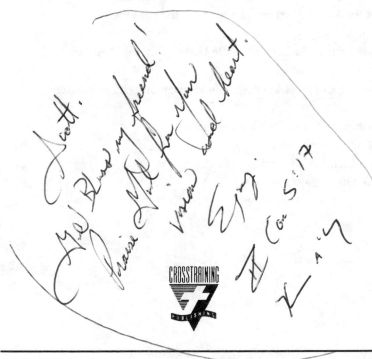

CROSSTRAINING
PUBLISHING

ABLE TO DREAM AGAIN

Keith A. Loy, Able to Dream Again

ISBN 1-887002-52-9

Cross Training Publishing
1604 S. Harrison St.
Grand Island, NE 68803
(308) 384-5762

This book is manufactured in the United States of America.

Library of Congress Cataloging in Publication Data in Progress.

Published by Cross Training Publishing,
1604 S. Harrison Street
Grand Island, NE 68803
1-800-430-8588

DEDICATION

To my charming wife, Kay,
for her unconditional love
and loyalty.

To Jordan Brooke.
Our little girl passed down from God.
Her abundance of energy
keeps me ever so mindful
of His faithful love.

I love you both very much!

ACKNOWLEDGMENTS

I would like to extend a warm round of applause to the following people. Their perseverance broke through the melee of finishing this project.

To my United Methodist Church family. Your belief in ministry and your action to get things done is overwhelming.

To the Worship Team. You continue to amaze me with your pursuit for Holiness. It is precisely this commitment that keeps us ever so present of His presence.

To my Sunday evening congregation. It gives me great joy the latitude that you extend allowing His longitudinal love to reach out and touch others.

Joel Engdahl. Our growing friendship has forever impacted my life. Your faithfulness in editing my elementary errors deserves more than a salute.

Barb Engdahl. Thanks for sharing a piece of your husband with me. Many long hours went into the editing wheel which kept us far from the doorstep.

Pastor Glenn W. Loy. Not too many children can share the respect that I have for you. You're not only my father but a true God-fearing man. Your humble heart deserves more than praise.

To the entire Frontline youth group. God bless each and every one of you for your warrior attitudes. The beat that you march to is priceless. The future rewards will be endless.

Dan Gaub. My friend. My Christian brother. You have given me more than I will ever be able to repay.

Ken and Barb Gaub. I take great pride in having such wonderful people in my life who are willing to tap into their personal resources to make this dream a reality. Thank you!

Shane Fruit. You have supported me in both word and action. You have been and island to me when the sea of this world is raging out of control. Thanks for introducing me to Gordon and putting this book in the capable hands of those who make dreams realities.

Gordon Thiessen. I recognize that most publishers never grace this page in a book. However, your leadership in this project and the gestures of friendship shared deserve a tip of the hat. Thanks.

The Wyatt family. Together we have crossed numerous rivers, climb many mountains and sat beneath a multitude of trees. I'm looking forward to sharing in more of life's adventures.

Larry Kroeker. For your constant encouragement and support throughout this entire project.

Finally, to the readers. I pray that this material will be well worth your investment as you pursue recapturing those lost dreams and restoring the vision.

Keith Loy

If you would like to write Keith A. Loy or have him speak to
your church or group, he can be contacted through:

UNITED METHODIST CHURCH
P.O. Box 916
Ogallala, NE 69153
(308) 284-8455

CONTENTS

FOREWORD

Keith Loy was a youth pastor in a midwestern town when we first met. His attitude toward life immediately attracted me. He and my son, Dan, soon became fast friends, so we maintained a contact. Keith has a fresh, young approach to an age old message, that of a positive Christian life. The book will hold your attention. It is easy and enjoyable reading, and is definitely worth your time.

Ken Gaub
Evangelist, Author, Comedian
Ken Gaub Ministries

INTRODUCTION

A disturbed and deeply troubled individual went to a psychiatrist to relieve his anxiety. He awoke melancholic every morning and he went to bed in the evening deeply depressed. His day was marked by darkness and clouds. He couldn't find relief for this anxiety. In his desperate condition, he decided to seek the counsel of a medical doctor. The psychiatrist listened to him for almost an hour.

Finally, he leaned toward his patient and said, "There's a local show at the theater. I understand a new Italian clown has come into our city and he's leaving them in the aisles. He's getting rave reviews from the critics. Maybe he is the one that will bring back your happiness. Attend the show and laugh your troubles away."

With a hangdog expression, the patient muttered, "Doctor, I am that clown."

You were that dream with promise, entertaining the crowds, moving to a rhythm of laughter, silly jokes, red juggling balls and a crazy entourage. Life seemed so bountiful–a never-ending sea of enjoyment, meaning and fulfillment.

Then from out of nowhere the cork was pulled from the washtub of lights and glitter and the drain completely swallowed up everything. The crowds began to dwindle. The sturdy pavement turned into muck. The helium lost its ability to keep you abreast of the situation. Little by little you sank into the mainstream of disappointment and misery. The drive was gone, the convictions stifled and the yearning crushed. Just another one of life's mistakes.

So many fit this category of despair and depression. Too many young people have relinquished the notion of a dream and have surrendered to the enemy of worthlessness. Numerous adults have forgotten the inner child that once gave them complete joy and true happiness.

"I came that they might have LIFE and have it ABUNDANTLY." (John 10:10b)

Jesus understood the need for fulfillment.

"Now to Him who is able to do exceeding ABUNDANTLY beyond ALL that we ask or think..." (Ephesians 3:20a)

Jesus developed a solution to achieve this fulfillment.

"...Good measure, pressed down, shaken together, running over..." (Luke 6:38)

Jesus gave everything He had for our fulfillment.

Life was meant to be "lived" not "survived." The unspeakable joy is at our fingertips just ready to be taken.

How do we face the raging demands with a determined delight?

How do we step back into the arena with a controlled pleasure?

How do we once again dream dreams and turn them into fervent action?

It is my prayer that the journey through the remaining pages will stir a long-lost passion, will kindle that dying ember and restore a sense of wonder. It's what God desires for you.

This life that Christ spoke of is not about where you have been but about where you are right now and where you want to go.

If your goal is to once again begin the voyage in search of undiscovered territories....then by all means, read on.

Let the games begin

---

*"My grace is
sufficient for you,
for power is perfected
in weakness."*

2 Corinthians 12:9

CHAPTER ONE

Have you ever beheld the opening day of the Winter Olympic Games? People, swarming into a stadium like buzzards to a carcass, hoping to glimpse their favorite athletes.

Athletes, tried and true, vie for their common goal. Men and women, who once visualized a dream, put it into hard work and sweat. Each one, having overcome incredible odds and obstacles, is now on the march to making those dreams a reality. These young minds, anticipating their greatest display of personal talent, are for now content with soaking up this brief incredible moment.

The crowds cheer. Flags wave. Bands play. All are taking in this prestigious wonder. Prayers are offered and speeches made.

Then the Olympic torch enters the arena. This commencement flame, this burning symbol of global unity, illuminates the new blanket of soft winter powder. The only sound is the perilous breath that rises from the embodied sea of people. The magnificent flame captivates every eye.

The fire ascends to the very top of the stadium. It turns to greet the crowd, the athletes and the entire world. It signifies unity. It portrays oneness and then there is a pause. The flickering light illuminates the night and places a peaceful glow across the faces of each member of its audience.

It is elevated toward the chalice.

A booming voice cries out, "Let the games begin," and the lighting of the Olympic flame passes into history, bringing the dreams and fantasies of these athletes into reality.

Most Americans have taken part in this world class event. We understand clearly its historical meaning for our universal globe of citizens.

Many of us have entertained dreams of someday walking the platform. We have in fact, lived it. We not only watched it on television but emotionally participated. Each and every one of us has had that moment of glory. We felt the thunderous applause after shattering world records. We shed tears during those bitter defeats. We stood there as they lifted into the rafters our symbol of patriotism: the red, white and blue. Tears poured forth like a river running rapidly through a mountainous terrain. We've been there. We have shared the spotlight. And like every champion, we had our moment in writing another chapter in the history books. It was our time in the spotlight. It was our front stage performance.

Then, something shakes the dream from reality. Suddenly we wake up and recognize our surroundings. Like a flash of lightning, it is gone. The room is empty. No anthem is being sung. Our chest only illustrates the comic character that we bought last year during the state fair. No medals. No fanfare. No homecomings will be made in our honor. Nothing. All is vanity. Just another dream that turns out to be a nightmare. Then, as many of us do, "we let the games begin."

Like a caged monkey, we recognize our limitations and learn to see freedom from inside the bars. We focus on our handicaps. We dwell on those limitations and repress the dreams that once gave way to determination and desire. We respond to this depth of discouragement and frustration by going back to the typical daily grind of drudgery. The goals that we once had, somewhere out on the horizon, won't get past the window pane. The visions that we once had, somewhere over the rainbow, will be placed by the trash at our own back door. We give up trying.

Negative truths about our limitations come whispering from the closet. Tales from the crypt of inhumane justice remind us of our inadequacies. Lies from the grave set us back from accomplishment. The abyss of failure lingers in our minds. These fallacies are accepted truths and become grave robbers.

Why do we spend profitable time in trying to measure our valuable worth against the performance standards of this world? It seems we spend more time trying to erect statues of our weaknesses than we do on our God-given strengths. We try to build castles on the sands of fantasy rather than with the bricks of reality. We place ourselves in the midst of a raging war of defeat when we should be living in the battle of spiritual conquest.

Hear these words of our Lord.

"My Grace is sufficient for you, for power is perfected in weakness." (2 Corinthians 12:9)

Scripture tells us that the Apostle Paul pleaded with the Lord three times to remove this thorn in the flesh. Paul called this thorn a messenger of Satan. This was not a simple expression for removal but a cry for help and a plea for mercy.

The Lord's reply was brief, "My Grace is sufficient."

Without being misunderstood, I think we need to shift our focus to work on our strengths and our own individual God-given gifts. Too many times we center our attention on our shortcomings and weaknesses but God has given each one of us divine talents of extreme importance. Since these glorious packages and faculties have been endowed upon us from above, it is safe to make a perfect assumption that they are flawless, perfect gifts. They are Heavenly stones that bear no fractures.

The flaws, however, lie within the recipient and not in the gift.

It is important for each one of us to lay hold of these tools and fortunes that our Savior has entrusted to us and build upon them.

As a young child growing up I chose that devilish road of finding my personal self-worth in the applause of an audience. My entire self-worth was balanced upon the cries of approval from my fans. The louder they cried, the harder I worked. The mightier the chant, the stronger I became. Passion, obsession, and selfish desire became household words that were written upon the walls of my mind, like graffiti sprayed profusely upon the downtown streets. I began auctioning my self-worth to buy the temporal self-satisfaction of becoming something I wasn't intended to be.

My situation clouded my vision of seeing my pointless future. My inner needs were stifled by my selfish wants. Trophies began robbing me of my true identity. Ribbons became my personal destiny. Medals held my fate.

Then the traumatic reality became an endless nightmare–the cries grew silent and the crowds began dwindling. I searched aimlessly for something to again build my self-worth and fill my inner void. My heart grew desperately thirsty and I was in dying need of being quenched, but nothing worked.

Many of us can relate to this senseless and needless way of living. I can attest to the painful hours that went into my careless way of living. I hope you see, however, that this is precisely the way the world feeds us. We spend hours filling our minds with numerous lies. Television and movie screens create false images about the external standards of this world. Countless movies, journals and advertisements teach us what is macho and acceptable. Minds buy into these fantasies and allow these obsessions to become realities. Our ears are plagued with destruction, violence and gossip. Our eyes are caressed with lust, sex and crime. Billboards, radios and magazines daily bend the truth and sow these seeds to a world which consumes them ruthlessly, a false hope desiring a better life. The sad part is that each one of us has experienced the destruction of believing these lies. We partake in the feast hoping it may be different for us. We gorge ourselves at the table of hell. We dine at the altar of despair.

The apostle John knew the emptiness that one finds in chasing the winds of the world.

In 1 John 2: 15-17, he wrote, "Do not love the world nor the things in the world. If anyone loves the world; the love of the Father is not in him. For all that is in the world–the lust of the flesh, the lust of the eyes and the boastful pride of life is not from the Father but is from the world. And the world is passing away, and also its lusts, but the one who does the will of God abides forever."

Your life is not a waste. It has been wonderfully made and beautifully created. God has given to each one of us spiritual wealth and treasures to be used according to His purpose. To this, we must be accountable. We must enhance their very worth and transform these talents into power. By demonstrating extreme care through meaningful sweat we learn what it means to conquer.

Many frustrations come not from without but from within. It has been said, it's not that which what lies behind us and it's not that which lies before us, but it's that which lies within us.

Too often our wish lists are filled with other people's treasures and not with our own God-given responsibilities. God created us with the divine purpose of building His kingdom. There are no mistakes. If you're not being you, then who is?

The world is filled with myths about having a profitable future and about living within those confines. But every road the world offers leads to a bottomless pit of loneliness, emptiness, frustration and pain. Deceit is man's way of success. Truth, happiness and love, however, are God's definition of spiritual wealth.

We may never physically stand upon a triage of blocks to receive a gold medallion for this wretched world to behold. However, we will receive an eternal medal of honor if we remain faithful to Jesus Christ.

An elegant day it will be.

We will have achieved the greatest potential that human minds and hearts can comprehend. An ecstasy of brilliance contains no greater reward.

His voice will softly resound, "Come into my kingdom, thou faithful servant."

Trumpets will ring out, celestial choirs will sing and the entire universe will stop to recognize our greatest achievement.

God gave us this earthly life so we could experience that wonderful day. Take heart, it's not over yet. Let's be encouraged by what God has given each one of us.

Loosen the grip of humanity. Rekindle those dying embers. Spark the forgotten fire. Set ablaze those gifts and talents. Let us be the people that God has formed and find those God-given bounties that will pave our way to a bright and wonderful tomorrow.

It is a wonderful life. Nothing else is like it.

Praise God!

Now, let His games begin.

The final frontier

---

*"I press on
toward the goal for the prize
of the upward call
in Christ Jesus."*

Philippians 3:14

CHAPTER TWO

A crack of lightning flashes across the distant sky. Thunder echoes across the endless plains. The man turns his head ever so slightly.

He laments, "It's going to be a mean one, Honey."

He's never been in this type of situation before. His face takes on the hard, punished look that the land has shared for thousands of years. Faithful lines are scarred deep within his brow.

He shifts his weight from one leg to the other. His hands dig deep within his pockets. His mind races back to those days when everything seemed so secure–the two bedroom house, warm beds, plenty of food to satisfy any man's appetite, a fine school for his children, a secure job with a promising future and not a care in the world. For a moment his face cracks into a simple smile.

A coyote bellows from the hillside.

But now he stands alone. The wagon is in such fragile shape. His oldest child has been fighting for her life for the last two days. The food has grown short. His cattle herd of ten has dwindled to seven. The horses are restless and the nearby storm has proven to be of little help. Fort Laramie is still a four days' journey away. The rain begins to fall a drop at a time.

"Better take shelter, Honey," he cautions.

"What have I done?," he softly whispers to himself.

He looks up into the sky which is slowly being taken over by the blackness of the clouds. The full moon slowly drifts into the darkness. The crickets grow more silent by the minute. Fireflies flicker. The mighty Platte River slowly moves by and a halo of fog mystically rises a few feet above its shallow banks.

He listens carefully to the sound of his breath and his heartbeat as it pounds ever so softly against his frail, thin body.

He has always believed that one should work hard, and yet, he has gambled everything in a game where the stakes are high. He has risked it all not knowing what lies in the cards of tomorrow.

There's no turning back now. He thinks of the future. His recalls his dream.

"That's it! The Dream! The vision of something better for my family." His voice carries strongly.

His shoulders begin to slowly readjust into their strongest position.

"The dream!" His eyes are no longer searching but a steel, driven passion fills his dilated pupils.

"The dream. That's why I've chosen this strenuous trip of hardship. I will endure. I will overcome. I will conquer." Strength fills his inner being.

"There is something more out there to create a better life. I must not forget my dream."

He is a man once more with convictions. Once again he steps toward his bucking stallion of life. He seats himself upon the saddle of chance and begins to spur his way to a better tomorrow—a ride of hope for the future. He then bridles his faith and gently turns the steed toward a lifetime of dreams.

We have all been on this quest for something better. Like a mountain climber who faces the challenge of the rocky ledge in hopes of reaching the peak's crest. Like an artist who turns a canvas into a breathless work of wonder. Like a musician who inquisitively places notes into fashionable order with a hope of someday hearing their melody played across the air waves.

But amidst our journey, have we lost the dream? Have we somehow given way to the daily grind without a purpose? Have we lost the meaning to our life? Does our life consist simply of walking aimlessly about while being tossed to and fro without intentions?

Stop and consider the past few days of your life. What has been the driving force behind the path you have taken? Maybe you can't even answer that question. We Americans have fallen into a trap of living without meaning. We want a quick fix for our economical devastation. We want more for less and much for little. We want things bigger, better and quicker with little or no effort. We have turned ourselves into a society of greed, manipulation and laziness.

We praise our forefathers for their sacrifices that we don't want to make for the next generation.

Each life that is born into this world has purpose and meaning. God gives everyone the capacity to live life with intention yet we choose a passageway of shallow living. We enjoy all the comforts that we can't afford and die hopelessly without reason. Credit cards are pushed to the limit where charging is habit.

The apostle Paul wrote three powerful verses in the book of Philippians.

"I press on toward the goal for the prize of the upward call of God in Christ Jesus. Let us therefore, as many as are perfect, have this attitude; and if in anything you have a different attitude, God will reveal that also to you; however, let us keep living by that same standard to which we have attained." (Philippians 3:14-16)

Ponder those words. Simply marvelous, aren't they? Paul understood clearly the significance of holding onto the dream. It is the engine behind the movement and the small but very powerful rudder that turns the gigantic ship. Paul knew that he must not lose sight of his earthly purpose of his Divine call.

First, Paul shares the important key that the goal must be an upward call. Every step in life must be spent in moving in the direction of the purpose. As we reflect upon the settlers' lives, we recall numerous days of hardship, disease, death and bewilderment. Setbacks were very common among the wagon trains. It didn't look very bright at the end of their tunnels. Things did not always appear to be moving upward.

What kept these voyagers moving westward?

The desire to reach the end. The will to see finished product. They didn't dwell on the barriers and hardships that littered the trail. They saw the finish line and proceeded to overcome those hurdles that were set before them.

The second focal point is attitude. Every day you are faced with a decision. Every morning you are given an option. With pen in hand, you begin writing another chapter into your book of life. No one else can do it for you. The election is held in your honor. As the rooster crows, so cries the dilemma. The choice is yours: triumph or tragedy, victory or defeat. Thus, your day begins.

Third, we must not give up ground. I am a die-hard football fan. Every fall my life takes on new meaning. Not too many things excite me like a tough, hard-nose played football game, especially in the college ranks. I heard a coach once say, "In this league of football, it's not always the better team that wins but it's the team who makes the fewest mistakes."

The team that makes the fewest mistakes! The game of football is simple. Outscore your opponent. This is done by taking more ground than giving up. We have been given a playbook, God's Word, that ultimately will take us across the goal line and keep our opponent, Satan, from ever scoring. The key is ground control. By investing ourselves in the playbook of life, we keep from losing yardage by bad decisions. That's what Paul meant by "living to that which we have already attained."

Many documents were written by our ancestors who took this journey west. Many pages are filled with those who questioned such a horrendous idea. Thank the Lord that many warnings fell upon deaf ears. Thousands made the incredible journey, dared the impossible and built the frontier. You and I have much to be thankful for as they paved the way. Sometimes I think we forget the battle scars, wounds and bloodshed that was done for our inheritance. The United States of America doubled in size due to these dreamers—those with a vision. The mighty Missouri River became the halfway point of a land that expanded to its new horizon and a new boundary, the Pacific Ocean.

Not every decision along our pilgrimage will look to our peers as profitable and heroic. Through the eyes of the Almighty, however, they are steps of promise and paces of power.

There will be pains, losses, failures and days of confusion as we board this ride and pioneer new horizons. We may encounter those who discourage our endeavors and dreams, but we must walk with confidence and conviction. We must not surrender when others find our realities as their unrealistic fantasies. We must boldly go where only One man has gone before.

Paul gave a command that must stand forever in the hearts of those who need meaning in their life. "Run in such a way that you may win." (1 Corinthians 9:24b)

Stop and consider what our ancestors laid down for us. Stop and consider what our Savior laid down for us. It would be sinful to give anything less!

We can make this journey through life with assurance and confidence. We can have meaning behind the race we run. We can experience joy, although hardship rings loudly. We can be content although pain lingers ever so presently.

Let me begin this chapter again. A crack of lightning flashes across your distant sky. Thunder echoes across the endless plains that are in your life.

All right, go ahead, it's your turn....finish your story.

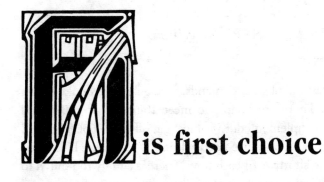 **is first choice**

---

*"It is not
those
who are healthy
who need a physician,
but those who are sick."*

Matthew 9:12

CHAPTER THREE

Reality. Days filled with demands. Schedules overbooked with appointments. There are people to meet, things to be typed and programs to be implemented. Kids must get off to school. The yard needs mowing and the house needs cleaning. There are bills to be paid despite the shortage of cash flow. There is simply too much to be done with little time to do it. Time just grows shorter and shorter. Reality.

Defining reality can simply be reciting a few recognizable universal life dilemmas. We have all quoted them. We have shared their frustrations and their triumphs. The question, however, still remains. What is reality?

Jesus Christ lived in a reality that simply didn't match society's expectations of the daily norms. He bucked the lifestyles of his audiences and upset their vigorous routines. He took the black road when man's way said to take the white. He went down when everyone else went up. He headed east while voices cried from a distance, "Go West." Why?

Stop and consider the disciples of the "Dream Team" that Jesus carefully put together. The ultimate coach was able to pick the very best. If you and I were given this chance, we would simply go crazy. Twelve of the best to be our very closest companions!

First, we would consider our needs. Talent, muscles and popularity would be key ingredients. We would stroll through the assembly line like children on a playground drawing up sides for their afternoon activities. The list could be endless. We all can think of those recognized by our society as the absolute best, imagine those who make a difference on a large scale. These are ones we would pick for our "Dream Team."

Jesus didn't take the obvious. He strolled down to the boating docks of orphans. He walked through the markets of adoption agencies. He rambled across the hillsides of the forgotten and the unwanted. He singled out the hated and the rejected.

One by one, Jesus pointed them out and said, "Come, Follow Me." Why? Didn't He know who these men were? He must have been having a bad day. Perhaps He just wasn't thinking.

But He was! He understood clearly. Jesus had the wisdom to discern what and who was needed to change the world. He knew the task at hand and pulled together His troops to get it done. He had perfect vision of absolute REALITY. Spiritual reality.

There is a story in the New Testament that portrays the bountiful care that only Christ could give in selecting His World-class Team.

The day had begun early for the Lord and grew into a hectic schedule of preaching, teaching and healing. Like a child discovering a new toy, the impetuous crowds kept the Savior busy. Every demand possible was made upon Jesus' life.

While teaching beside the Sea of Galilee an official from the synagogue came crying to Jesus, his heart filled with anguish. He entreated the Lord to give mercy to his little daughter who was at the point of death.

Let me take you there so you can experience this wondrous event and the thrill of being onboard with Jesus.

Christ is working his way through the hordes of people like a dull knife against a burnt steak. The disciples are doing all they can to keep the mob from swallowing up their friend. Their efforts are somewhat useless.

The intriguing pleasant gait of this crowd is becoming stifled and this once calm audience is turning into a mass of chaos. Every step must be in sync. To trip and fall would be a nightmare. This crowd is on the verge of a stampede.

Then all of a sudden Jesus stops and begins to look around. The crowd is silenced by this motion. Soft whispers start to move among these vultures.

Jesus then speaks, "Who touched my garment?"

A little laughter rambles its way through the numbers. Confusion plagues their thoughts.

"Jesus, You can see the multitude of people that are pressing in on You and yet You say, 'Who touched Me?'" Peter attempts to keep some composure.

But Jesus is persistent. "Who touched me?," He asks again.

The crowd is completely harnessed. Jesus begins to pick His way through the people. Every eye is watching Him.

"Is He mad? Is He frustrated? What is going on here?," the crowd queries.

These doubts fall upon the ears of the bystanders. Slowly he begins to remove all the questions on what He is focused.

He then diverts the last remaining individuals from crowding the path to His destination. Finally, everything is clear. Jesus is standing in front of a small domain with a few small timbered steps. Huddled at the bottom of the porch is a frightened old woman. Her clothing is tattered and stamped by years of employment. Her hair is tangled and matted, marked by days of torment and affliction. A tear loosens from her eye and begins to meander its way down her dusty cheek.

This woman is not of the norm. The prior twelve years of her life were of decay and pain. She had been ostracized by her peers. Her disease numbered her among the useless. She couldn't speak to anyone. She was labeled as trash and was treated accordingly.

Can you imagine? Twelve years of life spent in a world where the only conversation is with yourself. You are hated. You are spit upon. Your family has disowned you. Your friends consider you the lowest of the low and the ugliest of the ugly.

This woman had tried everything and everyone. She had nearly given up until a dim hope led her to Christ. Something told her that the crack of light at the end of this tunnel of disease was worth approaching. That tiny seed was worth planting.

It is important for us to understand that dim hope is always followed by bright strength. It's the tiniest of seeds that move enormous mountains.

She knew that this crowd would shun her and push her into the street if she tried to move toward the Savior. She feared the laughter. She dreaded the thought of raging insults. In addition she questioned her worthiness of such a miracle.

"Do I," she asked herself, "merit such a request?"

The thought of being cured outweighed the gnawing doubts. The idea of being cleansed crushed the lingering questions. The chance of being unblemished tainted the voice of uncertainty.

"If only I could get close enough to Jesus to touch His robe," she thought.

This determination made way for her finest hour. The horror of her loneliness subsided with that one touch of the Master's attire.

She wraps her ragged garb tightly around her tiny skeleton-like frame. Her tunic is bound carefully around her head to conceal her identity. She slowly picks her way through the close-knitted crowd. She can feel their bodies pressing against her as she carefully moves by. People are shouting the Savior's name as she pioneers this forbidden territory. She stops for a brief moment and cracks enough of the cloth to see those among the crowd. Her eyes hastily move from face to face in hope of noticing the Savior. She spots Him. His countenance is easily recognized.

"Just a few more feet," she says to herself.

She stretches her hand in the direction of Jesus and yearns that one miraculous touch.

She does it. She touches Him. Suddenly things begin to feel different. Her body begins to feel strange.

"Could it be?," she sobs to herself.

The mob grows quiet. The madness of the crowd is instantly tamed. Quickly she fumbles her way back through the multitude. She then crawls under the shabby staircase. Back to the familiar surroundings known to her as home. Trembling in joy, she sits quietly. She can't believe what has just happened.

Her entire life is about to change.

The voice is familiar. Apprehensively, she looks up. Her eyes meet His. He speaks very significant words that quietly rest upon the people. Words that will be branded upon their hearts. Everyone is taking part in this spectacular moment that will forever color the pages of our history books.

With His hand outstretched He softly and confidently says to her, "You are my first choice!"

Once again, Jesus is picking His Dream Team. He bucks the norm and looks into the forgotten ashes that once burned so brightly. He prowls those dungeons of tried prisoners. He walks into those outhouses of worldly life. He lingers in those painful shadows of disgrace and those profuse heaps of earth's garbage.

Jesus finds those in need and the heart that is thirsty. He searches for the child who will risk everything for that last hope of healing.

"It is not those who are healthy who need a physician, but those who are sick." (Matthew 9:12)

They are the ones who will grasp at a chance to be someone because they have felt the sting of being no one. They never doubt. They never waver. They have pure confidence in Him and Him alone.

It is this inner longing that makes them worthy for such an honor. This intense hunger that gives way to their miracle.

You are no different. That's why you chose Him. That's why He chose you. Jesus knew that He needed the very best to unfold His wonderful plan.

Let the breath of the Almighty fill your lungs. You are His first choice.

 saw quarters,
He saw Potential

---

*"The effective prayer
of a
righteous
man
can accomplish much."*

James 5:16

CHAPTER FOUR

I saw quarters, he saw potential.

I was just knee high to grasshopper when my grandfather passed away. I can't recall too many memories from the storage cellar of my mind but the mint condition quarters I will never forget.

Growing up in Nebraska made it extremely difficult to vacation in Michigan where my grandparents lived. However, when my family would make the pilgrimage across the midwest excitement permeated my heart.

Grandma would greet the family with the typical hug and common kiss. Of course, she never overlooked the dreaded pinch-cheek routine.

Grandpa, however, did something unusual and very special. He would stroll to the nearest chair and signal for each one us to venture towards him. He would pick us up and place us upon his knee. With one hand shielding our form from falling he would take the other and dig deep into his pocket. Somewhere in the well of his trousers, he would find a brand new quarter and secure it in our possession.

I saw quarters, he saw potential.

This was not grandpa's way of buying the love of his grandchildren. These quarters were not the change that can accumulate upon the top of one's dresser. They were brand new quarters displaying the current year of our visitation.

Grandpa made a very special effort of visiting his bank and procuring the vintage currency. These were gifts. Spiritual investments in my heavenly future.

I saw quarters, he saw potential.

For just a moment time would stand completely still.

Then he would put me back on the floor and off I would travel into that child's world of fun and fiction.

I saw quarters, he saw potential.

Often I think back to those special moments of receiving those quarters of love. Many questions invade my mind of what my Grandpa must have been thinking while I sat upon the altar of his knee. Something very transforming was taking place within that framework of a few moments.

I saw quarters. Twenty-five cents of pure candy. A little money that would buy me short term pleasure.

Grandpa, however, saw something more. It wasn't in the gift that he found such great pleasure but in the one who was receiving the gift. My life meant more to him than habitual living.

This was not a typical "glad to see you" gesture but a plea to the Almighty for my eternal destiny. While I was thanking him for this portion of measure, he was offering prayers for my spiritual asylum. While I basked in my new found treasure, he communed with God for a hedge of heavenly protection.

I saw quarters, he saw potential.

Every night before I envelope myself with covers and drift-off to never-never land, I quietly enter the room of our little girl. Curled up in a most extraordinary position is her small yet beautiful form. As I lean over the side of her crib, I can her softly breathing and filling the room with life.

I place my hands ever so gently on her brow and pledge her to Jehovah Jireh, the God who Provides. I dig deep into the well of prayer and offer her up to God.

This has become a very special time for her dad.

I'm sure that my presence is totally oblivious to her understanding, but to me it is a transforming event. To God it is life changing.

"The effective prayer of a righteous man can accomplish much." (James 5:16b)

This legacy that my grandfather gave to me is returned and comes full circle behind the doors of our daughter's room.

While she envisions sheep jumping the fence that only a child can see, I see the potential of a little girl. As she captures the imagination of a dream, I see the unfolding of a dream. As I try to capture her heart, I am confident that already she's captured mine.

Maybe someday I'll visit my local bank and request some off-the-press quarters. Though her eyes will see only a quarter, I'll except the responsibility of seeing her potential.

My Grandfather had a very peculiar wisdom about him that reached beyond human reason. When the occasion would arise for him to step into Christ's realm of living, a quarter would emerge and the minutes would linger. Each opportunity was seized by him. Each moment captured.

I may never really comprehend what took place so many years ago between the exchange of a smile and a quarter, but the heavenly rewards that have taken hold of my daily life will forever greatly outweigh that small token of carnal currency. To grasp the significance of that past blessing, I can only measure it upon the current unfolding of my gifts.

I saw quarters, he saw potential.

I'm so glad he did.

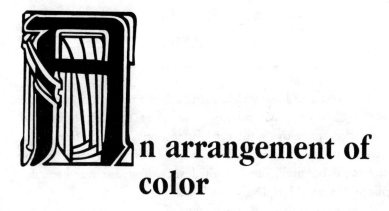

An arrangement of color

"For now we see
in a mirror
dimly,
but then face to
face..."

1 Corinthians 13:12

CHAPTER FIVE

Have you ever been walking through the mall on a wonderful peaceful afternoon? Meandering your way through hordes of people who are enjoying the same afternoon? You look from store to store wishing your credit limit could satisfy your inner wants. You behold bountiful displays of desires. You discover beautiful captions of wants. Helplessly, you walk on.

"Now what is this?," you ask yourself.

Picture frames filled in a wild array of random colors of tangled configurations. People are peering earnestly into the assorted collages. You wonder why. What value could be within these pictures of weirdness?

You move a little closer and consider the interesting formations. Your moment befriends you. A few participants move aside in defeat. You replace their position and begin staring into the picture. Your eyes fidget back and forth in frustration.

The caption reads, "Sea life."

"Now where in the world is the sea life?," you ask yourself.

Your mind cautiously reminds you how stupid you probably look. Somewhere there is a hidden camera recording this disgruntled event. You cautiously ask the young attendant what this is all about. She explains by telling you to look deep within the picture. There is more on the inside.

Finally, something begins to come forth.

"There! Right there!" You're pointing excitedly into the picture.

"It's a dolphin. In the left side of the picture. Oh, look everybody. There are more fish. Wow, look at the treasure chest."

You simply can't believe your eyes. It's incredible. You begin begging people to return. You also realize you are probably not making brownie points with those earlier quitters. So you quickly move to the next picture frame.

Spaceships emerge from the masses of confused color. You hastily jump to the next.

Dinosaurs fighting one another. Incredible. The minutes turn into hours. You can't take your eyes off these portraits of colorful ensemble. What a magnificent wonder.

Have you ever seen those colorful pictures that hold the 3D images deep within their bowels? Remember the anticipation that turned to frustration before the first picture developed? The inner longings flash to see the finished product and the passion to capture the final result.

Just imagine how many dreams and ambitions have failed simply because the author gave up. An insecure soldier turned into a meaningless sojourner. An insignificant credence burned up influential reliance. To give up is never digested by those who hope, have visions and dream dreams. They simply become destructive tools in mankind's pursuit for peace and spoil man's journey for a secure and stable mind.

We must not allow ourselves to be spiritually led into the tunnel of relinquished hopes and abandoned ambitions. How can we redefine the word laboring when the world has promoted a lifestyle of ease and manipulation? How can we re-establish a people that will find satisfaction through perseverance? People would rather take the easy road that leads to adversity in lieu of walking the impeded byways that construct triumph and victory.

Can we loosen the shackles of mankind's frail understanding of retarded efforts and constitute the realization of toiling through hardships? Can we finish the race that induces pain? How many Rembrandts' remain on their easels because the artist faulted in his plight to finish? Imagine the number of melodies that have failed to find favor with the human ear because the musician lost faith in his talent to consummate. How many inspiring works have been denied the opportunity to become a legacy to themselves and their ancestors?

Hardship and struggles have become something we all have tried to avoid, and we should, if a better road lies before us. However, what if the better road is the hard road? What if the only road is affliction? What if the road Christ ordained is simply pandemonium? What if?

Nowhere in the Bible did God say everything would be roses. Even so, roses still have thorns. We must find cause to endure. We must find a way to access the ability to carry on. We have to recognize our inner strength but can't limit ourselves to human understanding.

Can you recall those days of watching an infant prematurely attempt the art of walking? It begins as an immature balance of motion and a portrayal of being fuddled and tipsy. Relentlessly, the child tries and tries again. Numerous table corners implant themselves into the child's body. Bruises cover the infantile form and figure like a suntan clothing the skin of a beach bum. Over and over again the child presses on. Every thought, feeling and faculty is concentrated on this one endeavor. What drives the child to suffer through such continuous aches and pains? What lingers in the mind of these young creatures that causes them to hunger for such a bitter drink?

First, they learn how to crawl: the desire to move quickly from here to there on all fours. Pleasure is fulfilled by their new-found ability of mobility.

Second, they educate themselves in the art of standing: the knack of rising above their surroundings and seeing life from a different viewpoint.

Third, they begin the frustrating venture of walking, accompanying the convenience of moving about freely and easily with the absence of bruised knees.

Putting these qualities together with extra initiative, they begin their forward progress into adulthood.

This progression is an incredible task for these unripe and precocious species. Their journey is filled with monumental obstacles to endure and countless obstructions to overcome. With full determination they invest in this journey of growing up. This faith-walk moves with them into their adult lives.

God never said every road we walk would be painted with colorful flowers and vintage aroma. We will continue to face hardships and trials that will last throughout our earthly visit.

David wrote in Psalms 23, "Even though I walk through the valley of the shadow of death, I fear no evil; for Thou art with me."

He didn't say, "If I walk through the valley," but stated, "I will walk through the valley."

Our life channels were never intended to be worry-free but we have been promised that we will never have to walk them alone.

Why should we face the thought of giving up? Why should we ever entertain the idea of quitting? The same God who has the power to create storms has the same power to see us through the storms.

Sometimes you can tell when you're on the right track—it's usually uphill.

Face the incredible mountains. Take pride in the challenge of the cliffs. Find promise in the midst of the hurricane. Learn to stand boldly against the demands of this world. You won't stand alone. You will not run wearily and you can not be rendered powerless.

Mount those wings. You will make it through.

"For now we see in a mirror dimly, but then face to face; now I know in part; but then shall I know fully just as I also have been fully known." (1 Corinthians 13:12)

Imagine that darkest hour of Christ's life. He is surrounded by garden vegetation. His faithful friends are but a short distance away sleeping. His entire gown is soaked with sweat. His brow is doused with blood. His heart is being ripped with a pain He has never known before.

The perfect soul was wrenched with human sin. The utopian spirit was stained with our ugliness.

Jesus faced a pretty dark glass. He cried to His Father to wipe the pain away. He begged His Dad to remove the filth that was splattered across His window pane.

However, Jesus didn't give up. He didn't throw in the towel. He continued to search for meaning. He stared intensely into the frame of death until life emerged. This perseverance turned the obscurity of the cross into a crystal-clear resurrection. The dim taste of death for this King was overtaken by the distinct visibility of life.

Walking by faith is not easy. You and I face some avenues that look pretty bleak. However, it is this blind trust in the Savior that brings things into perspective. This hidden confidence in the Redeemer opens up understanding.

If we will endure with a righteous stubbornness and a immovable holiness, great rewards are in store. It's a promise. A sacred vow. A life back guarantee.

"Who will render to every man according to his deeds: to those who by perseverance in doing good, seek for glory and honor and immortality, eternal life." (Romans 2:6,7)

If you find yourself walking away from those paintings of colorful confusion, then you have given up on one of life's magnificent wonders. Beneath the calamity of hue is a mind-boggling sea of astonishment that will give way to hours of creative curiosity that will wet your whistle for more. Don't miss one of your greatest moments.

antasy playground

---

*"Let
no one
look
down on
your youthfulness."*

1 Timothy 4:12

CHAPTER SIX

I am the epitome of a fantasy playground. I have rivaled more NBA superstars in my driveway than you could ever imagine.

Weeds now probe through the cracks in the pavement but it wasn't that long ago that this driveway was one of the greatest fictional stadiums ever played. I can still see the old wooden backboard scarred with play supporting an old rusty rim bearing no net. A few shabby cedar bushes, some shrubs and the beat-up old garage door yet mark the court boundaries.

I can remember the board that was nailed to the post supporting the goal. I would use this piece of lumber as leverage to enable me to dunk the ball. A very important gesture when you want to be recognized in this game.

I displayed some of the greatest talent ever seen on this pavement of conscious invention. I would put on my favorite gym shorts, a weathered tank top and my Flash N' Dash tennis shoes. I just loved that pair. Then I would hit the court.

I would play for hours. Everything I shot at the hoop went in and if by chance I missed, I would call a foul. With a little imagination and my own play-by-play I could do absolutely anything I wanted.

I led the league in scoring and broke every rebound record ever tallied. I was simply amazing. Just me, the pavement, a hoop and a ball created an imaginary game of extreme proportions.

I was reminded of that playground while recently driving through a residential neighborhood. I saw a young boy creating his own heroic moment on his island of reverie playing roundball with his make-believe friends.

You have probably pounded this court yourself. Whether it's in your driveway or not doesn't really matter; but you, too, have probably drifted away from reality and entered this world of fun and adventure.

However, it's funny how our society strips those special moments from our memoirs and bars them from our show and tell. It robs them from our personal experience. To agree with society removes any thought of rekindling it's prize.

"Let no one look down on your youthfulness." (1 Timothy 4:12)

The Holy Word of God knew the value of this childhood sense of wonder in an amusement park of pretend. It is important to understand that those fantasy playgrounds don't have to cease to exist. Even during your adult years you can cross over into this invisible arena.

Dreams of this nature offer us so much. There are tremendous amounts of tools in our toybox of dreams if we would just open a drawer and take notice.

First, they give us possibilities and an endless amount of resources beyond our wild imagination.

Dreams are what you and I live for. The ladder of success is a dream of which we partake in hopes of reaching the final rung. Being a parent is a dream come true when we hear those cries echo through the delivery room. The Christian life is a dream to someday live in that eternal wonderland of perfection and peace. Dreams keep us alive. Dreams keep us anticipating what lies around the corner.

Second, they give us protection. A safe environment in which we can function righteously.

"Truly I say to you, unless you are converted and become like children, you shall not enter the kingdom of heaven." (Matthew 18:3)

This word "converted" in the Greek text means to be altered or changed. Life as a Christian is life in reverse. The earthly standard for an individual is to grow to a stage of being totally independent. Every child longs for that day to be distanced from the parental roof, to be rid of the rules and regulations that adults construct. However, Christians' goals are to live life opposite and to be dependent upon their Father. To totally trust in Him. Everyday,

Christians long to be more intimate and to be completely sheltered under the spiritual ceiling of God.

Third, they offer an inner peace. The calm assurance is knowing we are in step with Jesus Christ.

Every time I enter this arena of fiction I find myself completely oblivious to life's demands. It becomes a temporal escape to exercise joy and fulfillment.

Santa Claus does that for small children. Disney World shares with those who dare to enter its fortress. Why not allow your dreams to do the same for your own personal well-being?

Finally, they give us patience and perseverance to provide the strength to approach any situation with complete confidence and the ability to endure through any possible circumstance.

Don't allow human frustration and discouragement to cut off that once passionate wonderland. Your childhood fairy tales came from within your heart and imagination. Don't allow the external worldly forces to steal and kill that God-given territory.

Take time again to enter that fantasy playground. Put on your favorite shorts and grab a ball. It's the beginning of a new life and the restoration of that lost childhood sense of wonder.

John Keats once wrote, "I am certain of nothing but the holiness of the heart's affections and the truth of imagination—what the imagination seizes as beauty must be truth—whether it existed before or not."

I still love to play those games. I have never lost the joy in my imaginary playmates and realm of my fantasy playground. There is something very special about stepping into this domain.

The movie Hook, Hollywood's version, based on the popular children's book about Peter Pan, a boy who could fly by thinking happy thoughts, was very profound about this world of fantasy.

As the movie began to take shape Peter Pan was asked a very important question by his friend and companion, Tinkerbell, Tink for short.

"Have you forgotten all that you knew in never-land?"

Never-land was the fantasy playground where Peter and his

friends played. It was this part of the movie that Peter, now an adult, was faced with his most important decision, finding his way back to those days of make believe. This place known to him only in his mind. A place where he had joy. A place where he knew joy.

Maybe you have been wanting to step back through those doors to your playground. Once again, entering that arena of festivity held within your mind.

Those who dare to take the responsibility of such a gift will merit great reward.

Just one happy thought and you may find yourself rising above the world's hodgepodge on wings with vision and promise.

If Peter Pan did, so can you!

he thrill of victory
and the agony of
defeat!

---

*"I have fought
the good fight,
I have finished the course,
I have kept
the faith."*

2 Timothy 4:7

CHAPTER SEVEN

When Derek Redmond fell to the track, the crowd gasped with fear as he grasped his hamstring in utter pain. He had torn the muscle and was left crippled before thousands in Barcelona, Spain.

Never in his dreams did the 26-year-old Briton think that his Olympic bubble would burst with such closure. His cry echoed through the sentiments of each bystander. His agony would headline tomorrow's news.

He was the favorite. The athletic world had marked him the one to beat. He was the best. But it was all over now. His childhood fantasy had come to a bitter end. The thrill of personal victory was replaced by the agony of defeat. His country's anthem would never be embraced by his ears following his moment of victory. Everything had been completely erased from his mind when the muscle gave way.

It must have been the internal animalistic instincts that caused him to push away the medical team and begin the futile attempt of finishing. He knew that he didn't come to these games to be aided from the athletic field. He came to compete. He came to complete.

He stumbled to his feet as pain ripped through his body.

The original race had long been over and every member of the stadium was now focused upon Derek and his disappointment.

With anguish etched into his countenance and his entire body throbbing with an unfamiliar pain, Derek began the race of his life. What used to be a routine distance for him had now turned into a never-ending nightmare.

The first step was filled with terror as the agony vibrated through his body. The second step was the same.

Like a wounded animal fighting to escape the hunter, Derek hobbled on. Each step made it more and more difficult.

Then, from out of nowhere, his body was eased from the burden of walking. His arm was gently placed upon the shoulders of someone very familiar, someone capable of lifting the weight, Derek's father.

Together they made the journey to the finish line.

When they broke the plane of completion, the crowd roared with applause. This acclamation was not in jest but a cry of support and advocation. Not one dry eye beheld this drama of a a boy and his father's love.

One very important cross was carved that day into the minds of each bystander. It was best displayed across the chest and head of Derek's father, Jim. His shirt, now soaked with sweat and tears, proudly displayed the words, "Have You Hugged Your Child Today?" His hat triumphed the finishing touch with the Nike slogan, "Just Do It!"

So often we get sidetracked by the lack of results that surround our efforts. Dreams fall short because of worldly comparisons. Visions crumble for the sake of earthly analogies.

Listen to the words of the Apostle Paul.

"I have fought the good fight, I have finished the course, I have kept the faith; in the future there is laid up for me the crown of righteousness, which the Lord, the righteous Judge, will award to me on that day; and not only to me, but also to all who have loved His appearing." (2 Timothy 4:7,8)

Paul had a focal point. A theme that his entire life centered around. Nothing detoured Paul from finishing his race.

The Roman prison system couldn't offer him discouragement. The fruitless conduct of the church of Corinth left him with no despair. His personal thorn in the flesh allowed no room for personal hopelessness.

Paul had plenty of reason to cash in his chips of futility but his self-worth was not built upon worldly altars. Paul's attention was on Christ. His faith was built upon nothing less than God's righteousness.

Paul faced his challenges. He prayed through his obstacles that sometimes covered his passageways. He completely trusted God to remove all doubt that was set before him.

This race in life can get brutal. The highways will meander. Rivers will become treacherous. Pathways will develop potholes but the strength of our Beloved Savior can overcome anything that crosses our step.

Let me ask you a question. What is your focal point? What do you give the most attention too?

Too many people place their treasures, results if you will, upon earthly possession. They scratch and save to take hold of something that will someday be sold cheaply through their garage door.

Jesus didn't speak loosely when He said, "for where your treasure is, there will your heart be also." (Matthew 6:21)

He completely understood the human desire. Knowing that we all are born with a sinful nature, it is our natural instinct to crave worldly possession. However, when we are transformed by the Blood of Christ we have a new desire. A new focal point.

Nothing in this world can give satisfaction that will surpass this life than that of the saving grace of Jesus Christ.

Have the torn hamstrings left you disheartened and disillusioned about living? Has the pain left you disabled and paralyzed and given way to thoughts of giving up?

I have great news.

Has the terror of a broken relationship terminated any thought of attempting love again? Has the fear of death quenched the reality of abundant life? Have you given up in this plight for peace that surpasses all understanding?

I have excellent news.

Are daily schedules swallowing up your time for accomplishment? Are demands outweighing your efforts to complete important tasks?

I have wonderful news.

Seated within the arena of life is a Father who is just waiting to race to your side and carry the burden that has weighted you down. He longs to loosen the ties that render you helpless. He yearns to transfer the load from your shoulders to His.

Don't let the discouragement of worldly living blind you from seeing the true sense of life. Problems arise in this temporal arena. Uncertainties exist within the framework of human duration. Physical life is seasonal. It will come to an end.

Our God promised that we would not have to walk alone. He will shelter us through the storms. We will not simply finish the race but we will receive the crown of life by persevering.

Derek Redmond can argue the fact that triumph doesn't always exist in winning. He has laid upon the track beaten, bruised and alone. He has sensed the cold breath of despair.

God also can claim the fact that winning will always succeed those who endure.

he finishing touches

"Now finish the work,
so that your eager willingness
to do it
may be matched be your
completion of it,
according to your means."

2 Corinthians 8:11

CHAPTER EIGHT

The sad truth about our lives is that most of our dreams never get to a stage of development. We manage to destroy their existence well before personal sacrifice can enter the picture. We somehow lose the ability to see the dream as hopeful and crush its capacity in lieu of the obvious pitfall.

Teddy Roosevelt once said, "It is better to risk and have it checkered by failure, than not to try at all."

Jesus Christ shared the same sentiments concerning our gifts and abilities. He beckons the student to step out on the limb of venture rather than to hold fast to the trunk of complacency.

God has entrusted us with dreams and endowments during our earthly visit. We can't allow ourselves to be seduced by society in relinquishing them to their mediocrities. Open your eyes. Standing in the midst of your cornfield of lost dreams is a baseball field that will give way to thousands of memories. Right in the middle of your grains of frustration, discouragement and barren lifestyle are baseball diamonds of pleasure and enjoyment.

It is true that God is faithful to His children but he cannot bless what hasn't been entrusted to Him. He can't multiply what has not been placed in His care.

Many of us have entertained many different types of fantasies. We've imagined incredible fortunes and have tinkered with some pretty wild ideas. However, many of us have torched the image well before its construction.

Our fantasy worlds have been plagued with "if only." If only I had the ability to lead people this or that way. If only I had the money to go here or there. If only I merited such powerful positions I could tell people when or where. If only. If only.

"If only" is just one step away from being granted. It's the one inch shy of a new world record or the one second too slow in making the finals or that fraction of time in beating the clock. "If only" is that gigantic wall we build that keeps us from experiencing our dreams. Yet the truth of the matter is that wall is really just tissue paper that can be easily torn down. Many of us live in this failure of broken dreams and unachieved fantasies.

Over the fireplace in Fred Astaire's hearth is a souvenir, a precious reminder of this dancer's first screen test. The testing director sent it to his superior in 1933. It reads as follows: "Fred Astaire. Can't act. Slightly bald. Can dance a little."
Good thing it's a reminder in not giving up and not a memo of a dream that slipped away.

I believe it's another thorn in Christ's flesh when we settle for less, a scourge from the whip of inferiority when we chose to give-up.

You and I need to learn to finish what we start. We must master the art of concluding the God-given dramas despite the forecasts and not allow excuses to cloud our visions.

The apostle Paul was very pointed about finishing everything we start and completing every effort and attempt.

"Now finish the work, so that your eager willingness to do it may be matched by your completion of it, according to your means." (2 Corinthians 8:11)

So finish the race. Complete the exercise. Clinch the title. Fulfill the void. There is reason beyond our control to awaken the death of the dream and resurrect its fantasies. A dream cut short is a life cut off.

I do not want to confuse the issue of dream reality. Many of us have entertained dreams that ultimately will not happen. Age, circumstance and other situations simply will not allow our past fantasies to ever become tomorrow's realities. However, God is not in the habit of beating His children for past failures in accessing a dream. It is not His tradition to punish His kin for the lack of consummation of a desire.

When I was a child I shared the same dream with every other young boy in the state of Nebraska, the opportunity to play for the Cornhuskers. The years, however, have quickly caught up with me and the achievement of that wish has long been over. Time swallowed up that idea. They don't take players my age and they wouldn't want someone in my physical condition.

It is not my view that one should continue to desire such a futile idea of playing for the National Champions but it is my opinion that one should not live in the past and limit God to a stadium filled with thousands of fans.

God replaces lost dreams with new visions. He doesn't look back in the fog of missed chances. He looks over the horizon of tomorrow's opportunities. It is rainbow-living that God ordains in our futures.

If God gave you a mind to dream such wonderful notions as a young child, imagine what you can dream and do with the faculties of Spiritual maturity.

Don't see your dreams as small and unimportant to God. In that light, everything that man does is pretty tiny compared to a God who holds the universe in the palm of His hand. Don't measure your self-desires against that standard. God just loves His creations and nestles within us the ability to dream and the power to see them through.

Peruse around the attic of prehistoric passions. Go open the garage door that houses boxed-up desires. Descend the stairs to the basements of forgotten dreams.

God wants you to finish what you started. He doesn't want you to give up and disclaim those wonders to a world that enjoys destroying them. He doesn't want you to waiver in bringing them to their fullest potential. Make room for these treasures in your heart.

It's the icing on the cake. It's the cream that rises to the top. It's the finishing touch.

The beatitude of attitude

"Blessed
are the pure
in heart,
for they shall see
God."

Matthew 5:8

CHAPTER NINE

It could have only come from a fairy tale.

The rays of the sun gracing the brow. The ocean waves providing music as orchestrated by the tide beating against the sand. The refreshing coolness of lemonade waltzing down the pipes of one's throat. Seagulls ornamenting the cloudless skies. Palm trees painted against the canvass of abundant and animated vista.

Everything is completely peaceful. No worries. Nothing stewing upon the stove of life. No storms lingering on the horizon.

Just surrounded by total bliss.

Wouldn't life be wonderful if everything that we experienced was encased in the above graceland?

Even more important are the wonderful attributes exhibited when our attitude harbors this very nature during crisis and unsettling circumstance.

We all enjoy those peaceful feelings that go along with routine agendas without those hideous and inconvenient worries. We covet the nature of serenity minus the catalogue of grief.

You and I can possess this relaxing treasure by recognizing that the response to an incident evolves from the inside out and not from the outside in. This response is attitude.

Dr. Victor Frankl exclaimed boldly that the last of human freedoms is attitude. Each one of us has the ability to choose attitude in any given circumstance.

We cannot control the storms that linger upon our horizons and the clouds that overshadow us with heartache. However, we can control our attitude in reply to any given dilemma.

We sometimes confuse this issue by blaming the surroundings for the attitude expressed. We point our finger in justification in an attempt to rationalize the unsettled emotion. We often blame the tide for the shifting of our internal sands. We even go so far as to accuse the devil for our shortcomings and misguided actions.

Attitude is something that awakes every morning along side us beckoning a decision. Every thought expressed and every action displayed is in direct correlation with the attitude felt.

Like a container of cold water placed in a pan of boiling water, we must learn to keep the temperature on the inside cool and relaxed though the immediate surroundings are stewing with heat.

There is an art to achieving utmost integrity by recognizing an inner battle, confronting the internal foe and taking the proper steps in healing and restoration. Don't allow society's voices and temporary statues keep you from firming the foundation within.

The world sows lies of deceit. The agenda is to persuade you in explaining away your faults. God's way is truth. We must turn those shortcomings over to Him and allow His sovereign grace to change a character flaw.

This humility is tough. To show weakness in a world that highlights strength is hard. To demonstrate frailty when muscle is the message is difficult. To swim against a current of power when fragility is ever present is tough.

However, by taking this risk and stepping into this unpopular arena of change, you have overcome a hurdle that will forever reward your life. The final result is strength in character with a positive attitude.

Is it worth it?

No matter what comes your way or what overshadows your bed, you will endure with great perseverance and supreme confidence.

I guess attitude is a beatitude!

Blessed are those...

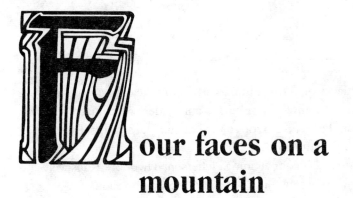 **our faces on a mountain**

*"You shall love
the Lord your God
with all your heart,
and with all your soul,
and with all your mind."*

Matthew 22:37

CHAPTER TEN

Four faces on a mountain. A perfect replication carved into the arduous rock known as granite. Four leaders recognized for their patriotism. Four men who had a dream and diligently labored ensuring its completion.

Abraham Lincoln, Thomas Jefferson, Theodore Roosevelt and George Washington. Guys with grit. Men with vision.

You can see this mammoth mountain amidst the whispering pines of the Black Hills in South Dakota. This historic place is known as Mount Rushmore. People come from every walk of life to gaze at this majestic carving.

The first glance reveals a breathless undertaking. A massive portrait painted against the endless sky towers above the plains.

Upon a second closer glance, cracks are revealed. They meander like tributaries across a landscape as they tarnish the monumental faces. Giant scars blemish the visage.

These battle wounds represent more than erosion but also symbolize a nation that is decaying. These leaders tilled earnestly the very soil that we litter. Forefathers breathed the very air that we ungloriously pollute. Stellars crossed the rivers that are now becoming sewage dumps and flowing trash pits. America has simply become a nation filled with cracks.

This nation, once unified in a call to create all men equal, has turned toward discriminatory acts. Equality to all human life has failed to be unconditional. Justice has fallen to greed. Liberty has been twisted for selfish gain.

People are standing with outstretched hands to fill their own personal pockets of happiness. The cry of the needy grows steadily louder while the dance of the rich grows increasingly stronger. Children are sacrificed for easy convenience. Responsibility has simply grown weak and our playgrounds have now become battle-fields of violence and murder.

What's next? What is the answer? What can any one person do?

These questions are not new to us. For years they have drifted through the alleys of our minds and have infested our gutters of thought. Like the common cold they will forever stuff up our breathing and ache at our muscles. They sever our joints and incubate poverished living. While this plague moves through our society like a thunderstorm across the western plains, we remain comfortable.

We lounge in our easy chair with the remote control and just erase the problem by flipping a channel. If we can't find an appropriate program to establish focus, then we turn to blame—the education system, the government, the church or other sorts.

The cure, however, is simple.

Maintenance. Care and subsistence. Daily exercise. Proper eating habits. Appropriate sleeping practice. Routine living. It is this mixture that is used in building His kingdom.

Too many structures have fallen from lack of care. Monuments have crumbled due to poor regard. It's critical to understand the validity found in concerned supervision. In business, it is excellent buying and spending practices. For a coach, it is proper conditioning and play execution. To an athlete, it is lifting technique and a well-rounded diet.

For a Christian, it is no different. Maintenance is the rudder that directs the gigantic ship and the bridle that controls the high-spirited horse. It is the very essence of the Christian faith.

Poor maintenance is like a cistern with a hole in it.

I know a gal who has tried every diet known to mankind. She probably owns every book ever written on the subject. To the best of my knowledge she hasn't lost a pound. The longest she ever stuck to a diet was less than two weeks.

Many of us live our Christian faith by these same standards. We want instant results. We want to see that our labor is bearing fruit. Eventually, we get tired. We become lazy. We harbor excuses. Ultimately, we give up.

We want the fullness of Christ yet we get satisfied with the smallest of appetizers. That's a great way to begin a meal but we can't simply stop there. We would miss the main course.

Nourishment was never intended to come from the horsd'oeuvres. The same holds true with Christian living. You may have had your spiritual whistle moistened by a sermon, a song, a concert, church camp or some other form of ministry but it was only to entice you in preparation for the main course.

It's important that we learn to be able to separate the relish tray from the the meat dish.

Are you one of those Christians that sits in a church pew and finds satisfaction through your emotions? Do you grovel for days if the message failed to lift your spirits? Do you measure your Christian growth against your human senses?

God is not a feeling but a fact! He is not a passion but a principle!

Can you grasp that?

Wrestle with it. Tussle with it. Believe it! This powerful substance is the marrow of true Christianity.

Many feelings and passions can come from the facts and principles but they must be in that order. Becoming Holy doesn't always feel good. It can be a very painful process. We can't keep going from mountain top to mountain top looking for a spiritual high.

Imagine what our society would become if the only thing eaten was anchovies. Though to some anchovies are the epitome of delicacy, it cannot be one's total diet.

It amazes me how many people sit within our own congregations spiritually stagnated and dull. The only thing that keeps them from being labeled as a spiritual corpse is the heartbeat that you find when you take their pulse. They have come to church for so many years their pew has a gold plate with their name stamped upon it.

Some of these folks, however, don't have a compassion for the lost. They are not even convinced that Jesus is the Savior. They get bitter and angry when change comes about. They are the ones that quarrel over hymnal colors and neglect the gospel message of love.

I don't want to give you the impression that I am downing the old guard of the church. Their faithfulness is something to be praised. If the church is going to make an impact in our society, however, this faithfulness needs to result in growth. The loyal membership needs to be turned into meaningful maturation. This show of attendance needs to be accounted for in hands extended outward because of brotherly love and not a finger pointing in judgment.

Jesus commanded only two things. "You shall love the Lord your God with all your heart, and with all your soul, and with all your mind. This is the greatest commandment. The second is like it, You shall love your neighbor as yourselves. On these two commandments depend the whole Law and the Prophets." (Matthew 22:37-40)

This love comes only through maintenance. A daily dose of prayer, conversation, Bible study and fellowship with our best Friend. We can't go from Sunday to Sunday and expect to grow. We need a consistent diet. This is how we learn to love God with all our hearts and to walk with Him with all our soul. To understand Him with all our mind, we must hunger for God until we are stuffed and then continue eating.

When a cup is full and you continue to pour, it is not what is in it but what overflows from its brim that makes the mess.

The same applies to our lives. The same applies to Christ's commandment. If we take care of number one by loving the Lord God with ALL our heart, soul and mind, the second will follow. It just happens.

By learning to love God, we simply begin loving our neighbor. When we feed ourselves from the table of God we begin to have a hunger for the lost. We learn to fight fire with love and hurl careful words of peace at those who offer up insult. We must confront with arms of understanding those who delight in being mean.

Heavenly damage is done to the adversary by learning to respond completely contrary to what the world expects!

We need to rid ourselves of our natural human approach of reacting and learn to see the power in responding. Love packs an enormous punch. The blow leaves the foe in utter dismay.

Don't let this world rob you of quality time with the Lord. Keep from schedules that burglarize your prayer opportunities. Stop the cycle that has rioted against your Bible study and has stunted your growth.

Sure, there are cracks that ramble across this nation. Clefts are still destroying the sod. With careful maintenance, however, we can make a difference.

"You therefore, beloved, knowing this beforehand, be on your guard lest, being carried away by the error of unprincipled men, you fall from your own steadfastness, but grow in the grace and knowledge of our Lord and Savior Jesus Christ." (2 Peter 3:17,18)

Daily maintenance.

You can read in the second book of Corinthians that your careful maintenance results in the spreading of God's message. Personal Bible Study, continuous prayer and positive fellowship never return void. These items, taken from God's basic food groups, build more than the body stronger, they impact the entire world.

Four faces on a mountain. What do they mean to you?

t's supper time

*"I tell you the truth,
unless a man
is born again,
he cannot
see the kingdom of God."*

John 3:3

CHAPTER ELEVEN

King David had become one of the greatest leaders of all time. Revered for his leadership. Respected by his foes. Regarded for his throne. He was a powerful man and a mighty ruler. He was graced with intelligence and commissioned by God Himself. It's no wonder David wore his colors proudly.

However, David wandered across the boundary lines of stability and voyaged into the pitfall of lust. His eyes caressed the naked body of a young woman, Bathsheba, and in a puff of smoke David found himself seduced into a cavity of passion. Sin wrought his soul. Immature greed plagued his heart.

As days passed into weeks word came to David that his sin had produced the seed of a newborn child. David's sin led to another crop of deception—chicanery. By manipulating his faithful soldiers, he ordered the death of this woman's husband, Uriah.

Imagine the dilemma of this powerful king. With a wave of his hand he could command thousands to raid and terrorize nations. With a single word, commission soldiers to take their own lives. His authority was known by all and challenged by few. He was one powerful dude.

David could have forfeited his personal relationship with the Father. He could have auctioned his soul off cheaply to his fans and they still would have stood by his side and continued worshiping the very ground he walked. He could have orchestrated a concert of selfish deceit for his audience and they surely would have come to a standing ovation following his phony performance. What futility that would have been.

David knew he could not cash into the temporal riches of society. He would not pay the piper to play a softer lullaby filled with subliminal messages of facade.

Many of us have faced a similar lifestyle. We've hidden behind false impressions. Behind closed doors we secretly invent ways to get those things we selfishly want. Lies are embroidered, stories are misrepresented and truths half-told. We see the rewards outweighing the spiritual perjury. We continue varnishing the finish while the wood still rots below. We continue flaunting our needs and ignore the infection underneath. Like an impostor, we survive by being someone or something else. We become fiction. We become counterfeit.

There's much to be said about those who dabble in this misconception and people who ribbon in forgery. However, this chapter is not about the consequences of fraudulation and deception. The theme is about forgiveness and God's response to a repentant heart.

God had other plans for David.

David now faced his ultimate battle. His greatest foe. This conquest held more for David then any lion or bear he had wrestled. This made his Goliath ordeal look pretty small.

A prophet was sent to confront David about his sin. That's the wonderful thing about our God. He never let's his children live in their sin.

David faced his sin. He wanted a better tomorrow. The restless nights were beginning to get the best of him. I'm sure he was exhausted with all the misleading stories of Uriah's death.

David wanted a purified heart. David humbled himself and cried to God for cleansing. He dove into the healing waters of God's grace.

The story doesn't end there though. The beautiful ending is not found within David's cry for forgiveness but in God's response to his plea.

Listen.

"Then David comforted his wife, Bathsheba, and went in to her and lay with her; and she gave birth to a son, and he named him Solomon. Now the Lord loved him and sent word through Nathan the prophet, and he named him Jedidiah for the Lord's sake." (2 Samuel 12:24)

Wow! Did you get that?

The answer is found in Solomon. His sovereign love directly resulted in this newborn baby. What a portrayal of total amnesty. Out of the adulterous mess would come the lineage of Christ. From the bed of sin would come the forebears of Jesus. Conceived from the relationship of murder would be our Savior. Joseph's ancestry dates back to Solomon. Our Saviors earthly father had Solomon's blood.

Forgiveness goes a long way when it's in the hands of God.

It's simply incredible. That's a forgiving God. A true loving Father.

This front line picture is simply incredible. God looked down upon David and saw his authenticity and responded far beyond David's comprehension. Beyond anyone's comprehension. It's just like our God. When we take one step, He takes two.

I can see God talking to David.

"David, I just want you to know how much I love you and forgive you. Always know, my child, I will never leave you nor forsake you."

"I'm going to do great things for you. I want to demonstrate my true love for you. Your next child will be a boy. His descendant will parent the Savior of the world."

"You see, David, I truly love you! I do forgive you!"

Can you hear God talking to David? Can you hear God speaking to you?

You may be living in a romance of lies, distrust, deceit, brokenness, despair and sin. God, however, can turn the tables on you. He can restore a life to heights far greater than ones thought possible.

God is not in the business of simple restoration but in abundant living. His joy is found in giving a person more than they feel worthy to receive. He just loves to out give his children. He delights in going overboard with his kiddies.

It's time to step back across those dividing lines of worthlessness and begin walking once again in the pastures of prosperity. You've been lurking around in the shadows too long.

You have been lingering in the alleys for no reason. Like the prodigal son you've been wanting to come home. Like the prodigal son, it's time to come home.

It's supper time.

Has the soul been aching for nourishment? Has the sin drained your energy supply? Have the failures vanquished your inner strength?

Come home.

Has the cancer rendered your extremities useless? Has the disease completely destroyed your body? Does breathing take effort? Is blinking a chore?

Come home.

Has a failing relationship ripped your heart in two? Has the home given way to pain and disappointment?

Come home.

Have you been wanting to give up? Have you been telling yourself that nothing is worth living for?

Come home.

The table has been set. The meal has been prepared. The porch light was never turned off. Step from the darkness and into the light.

Don't worry about knocking. There's no need to ring the doorbell. Please, come in. A feast is being held in your honor. A banquet of restoration for abundant living.

You are finally home.

It's supper time.

 ather like daughter

---

"For you have not received
a spirit of slavery
leading to fear again,
but you have received
a spirit of adoption
as sons by which we cry out,
'Abba! Father!'"

Romans 8:15

CHAPTER TWELVE

It was a typical autumn afternoon along the mighty Mississippi. The waters pleasantly moved by. A whippoorwill sang from a nearby oak. Cattails danced in the slightest of breeze. Bullfrogs croaked from the surrounding lily pads. A riverboat was making its way up the river. Its paddle wheel thrashed the muddy waters with smoke rising from it's stack. A perfect setting for a Tom Sawyer adventure.

The old man had been watching her for quite some time. He was enjoying her feminine innocence. Her golden hair glistened in the hot rays of the sun. It reminded him of days gone by when he was just a boy.

She was a young lass around the age of ten. She loved to walk along these waters. She'd been doing it for years.

Every so often she would stop and remove her sandals. She would sit along the bank and let her feet dangle in the water.

She loved to bask in the wildlife of nature and watch the boats go up and down the channel.

Suddenly, she began to wave her arms erratically and call out to the approaching riverboat.

"Over here," she shouted. "Come over here and pick me up."

The old man was amused by this sudden outbreak. He tried to help the little girl by sharing some personal wisdom.

"Little miss. That riverboat can't stop here. There's no dock for it to port."

He chuckled.

"It just won't stop here."

The little girl ignored the old man's remarks and continued to call out to the riverboat.

"Come over here. Come and pick me up!" she cried.

The old man once again was humored by her suggestion. He tried to speak to her once again.

"The boat will not stop. It never has and it never will."

Again she shunned the old man's comments and continued to jump up and down.

To the old man's surprise the boat began to slow and ever so carefully turn toward the bank.

The little girl smiled.

The riverboat slowly positioned itself. The little girl was excited and stood watching with great anticipation. She could hardly contain herself.

The portal was lowered and at once the little girl began to skip up the plank. Just as she stepped onto it's bow the old man called out.

"Oh, little girl! Little girl! Please tell me. How did you know that the boat would stop here to pick you up?"

"That's easy," she said. "The captain's my daddy."

She turned and with confidence disappeared into the captain's quarters.

I fell in love with this story the first time I heard it told. I was delightfully moved with its strong message of the perceptive knowledge of father. The confidence found in the security of recognizing dad.

Our little girl, Jordan, is beginning to pioneer the English language. Even though her first two words are common among this voyage, they are still pleasant to hear.

Mama and Dada.

The two most important people in her life. Her two very best friends that enjoy her company.

It's no wonder I love to hear her giggle when I put my lips on her naked belly and blow. To hear her laugh when I pretend that I'm a bucking horse and J rock her up and down. To watch her snort when I toss her in the air and set her down on the floor. (The snorting she got from her mother).

I love my daughter. Her voice has captured my entire attention.

Her existence has seized my whole being. Her joy has taken my love prisoner. There is something very special about being her parent.

The same is with our heavenly Father. He is entirely wrapped up in our living. His love toward us cannot be measured by our limited understanding for He finds great reward in His creations. His love knows no bounds. It is not overshadowed by worldly emotion. It is not limited to human comprehension. He simply loves us. God finds something very special with being our Parent.

It's hard to picture a God rolling around on a floor with His children, playing catch in the backyard with His sons or laughing and giggling while playing Barbie. Many of us cannot relate to this kind of God. We can't imagine this sort of relationship.

He loves to build sand castles in the backyard box, jump up and down on the trampoline or hang upside-down on the jungle-gym. Sliding down the slipper slide gives Him great pleasure. Swinging around the merry-go-round is an enormous thrill.

Our Father is a God who basks in the laughter of His children, thrives on screams of joy in His friends and finds luxury in the cooing of His kids.

Playing marbles, jumping rope and kicking the can are moments never forgotten in the heart of our Daddy. Singing songs, telling stories and hide-and-go-seek are forever branded in the mind of our Father.

It was our Spiritual Father who invented the high-five. He drummed up the words, "awesome, cool and hot stuff."

He loves His children.

Have we confused the power of the Most High with memorized prayers, church membership rolls and fashioned liturgy? Have we lost Him amidst the stained glass, choir robes and colorful hymn books?

Somehow we have come to believe that the Almighty is a judge that is waiting to pound His gavel and deem us unworthy. That He is a prosecutor looking for the smallest infraction to indict us.

God granted each one of us, however, the personal right of

becoming heir. The honor of becoming family.

God doesn't call us "servant" even though that is precisely what we need to be. He didn't request us to be only a friend, even though that is what we hope to be. He calls us child, for that is what we are!

He's our Dad. A perfect, flawless, supernatural Dad. A hero.

"For you have not received a spirit of slavery leading to fear again, but you have received a spirit of adoption as sons by which we cry out, 'Abba! Father!'" (Romans 8:15)

Jesus Christ signed, sealed and delivered the entire adoption papers with His precious blood. No custody battle took place. No lawyers were hired to wrestle over who's the most powerful. The jury was never assembled. The case was never opened.

The judge was God Himself. He presided and declared you not guilty.

Take His hand and walk from the courtroom.

It's that simple.

The birthing canal

---

*"If we confess our sins,
He is faithful and righteous
to forgive us our sins
and to
cleanse us from all
unrighteousness."*

1 John 1:9

CHAPTER THIRTEEN

"Your turn," she says.

The thought is almost unbearable. Every excuse known to man scrolls through your mind.

"It's four o'clock in the morning," you try to quibble, but the rationalization falls incredibly short.

You slowly pull back the covers and make your way down the corridor. The hall resounds the cry of a young, impatient and rude little creature. Your mind beholds the echoes of every off-key note that the child makes.

You enter the room. The air is filled with a very distinct aroma, the fragrance recognizable to any human nose. You turn on the lamp. The illumination gives off a soft peaceful glow. Like peeling an orange you gently unwrap the little gift carefully not to hurt the inner fruit.

Once the wrapping is removed you begin the routine process of changing the diaper and preparing another bottle. While rocking the child to sleep, you hum another soft melodic lullaby.

The minutes brush by and you place your own head against a pillow and drift off to dormancy, knowing that somewhere out in the night a small voice will break the silence and beckon your encore.

What a joyous chapter written in our ongoing book of life. This whole miraculous stage of childbirth and development is very powerful. There is so much we can learn as we share in one of God's most awesome miracles.

Have you ever imagined what this young child goes through?

Every step during those nine months of growth are precisely planned and delicately laid out. Surrounded by a soothing liquid mass of darkness the child receives everything it needs–a constant food supply to build its body healthy and strong, a warm environment that completely shields the baby from any negative interference and the music of a strong heart that the baby grows to trust and cherish.

What a life! Every need possible has been completely covered and met by our beloved Creator.

That's something you can always bank upon. God provides the answers before we have the questions. God supplies the need while we still hunger for the wants.

Then something begins to tear down those faithful walls of comfort and support that this unborn child has known. The pillars of a stable environment begin to crumble. A pressure begins to mount against the tiny skeletal frame. It's body is pulled and pushed. It's entire known world is completely destroyed. Never is the child asked for it's opinion nor suggestions taken on it's behalf. The only solace this child will find is the brand new experience of life as we know it today.

We too get sustained in contentment. Like the fetal stages of an infant we bathe in the warmth of serenity. We eat from an abundant food source. Besides a few good kicks to keep our Master ever present of our existence, everything is perfect. All is well at our doorstep. Bills are being met. Grades are being made.

Then all at once, boom!–a bombshell is dropped. Something triggers the land mine. The once quiet world turns into utter chaos. The boss is thankful for the years of dedication and service but inflation is forcing him to cut back his personnel. A dreaded phone call is received with news that your husband will not be returning home. Your fifteen-year-old daughter is soon to be a mother, a best friend has AIDS, the car has been totaled and the insurance company is now dropping your policy.

Everything is unglued. We try desperately to grab hold of something to stop the painful fall, but our efforts fail and the tension heightens. The winds continue to blow. The hurricanes destroy. The tornadoes forever change our world.

We've all been through this monstrosity of affliction. This enigmatic cycle of conflict.

We ask ourselves over and over again, "Why is this happening to me?"

The pains of childbirth are something to behold. I will never forget the jubilation that rushed through my entire body as I held my new little girl. I couldn't believe that this little creature that was sheltered from the storms of life inside my wife's womb was now present in her full wonder.

Little Jordan Brooke. Our blonde, blue-eyed adventuresome little terror. (I have to admit though, I love it.) The wait was completely over. The labor pains were drifting off into never-never land. All the suffering that tarries with the birthing process was being replaced by total joy.

I'm sure the child's experience is much the same. With the complexity of the birthing process now over, the child undergoes this new life filled with lights and images. Those familiar voices now have faces. The dark, never-ending nights have turned into radiations of unique colors.

The old is gone and the new has come.

So it is with the birthing process of a Christian. The spiritual pains that go along with being "born again." When you and I give our hearts to the Lord Jesus Christ, much is required.

Like the importance of the child's positioning during childbirth, our head also needs to be in the right direction. We have to come to the Lord with a genuine heart and a truthful mind. This can be very painful. Exposing sin is nothing to be enjoyed until we see the end result. Salvation.

Listen.

"I tell you the truth, unless a man is born again, he cannot see the kingdom of God." (John 3:3)

When one comes to Christ, this process of entering the spiritual birthing canal is inevitable. You can't bypass this door. You can't jump to go and collect the two hundred dollars. You must enter the canal.

So what does it mean to enter this tube, this salvation tunnel which cannot be avoided?

The Bible says in Romans that we all have fallen short of God's glory. No one is good enough. That's painful in itself. Especially since man struggles with admitting failure. You and I have to come to grips with the fact the we do not deserve eternal life. We will never merit such an honor through our own efforts. You can't labor your way into heaven. It is by the grace of God.

This grace is what bridges the gap between life and death. When disease plagues your heart, grace is the cure. When loneliness echoes through the corridor of self, grace is your friend.

So how can you and I possess some of this grace and own a ticket to this eternal ride?

Listen.

"If we confess our sins, He is faithful and righteous to forgive us our sins and to cleanse us from all unrighteousness." (1 John 1:9)

Humility is tough. All those sins we've hidden for years under our garments of human acceptance must be revealed. The soiled laundry can no longer be stored in the corners of our hearts and the closets of our minds. It must be unveiled. The mask has to be removed. The front has to be torn down. The bond has to be broken.

Do you see the sting in entering this canal? Can you feel the pangs that go along with being "born again"?

It's no wonder so many people buy into religion instead of the relationship of Christ. They choose pleasure instead of peace and death in place of life. They option to stay numb to the Holiness of God due to their self-righteous indignation. They would rather find man's acceptance than God's repentance.

However, the eternal result is not worth the temporal worldly standards of survival. The price will forever outweigh what we thought the product was worth.

We have a Father who longs to free us from the chains that tie us down and the shackles that keep us from His spiritual liberty. It's no wonder we call Him Messiah.

Oh, the joy that floods my soul every time I think of our little girl. Yet, I'm reminded of the love my wife and I have for our daughter cannot compare to the love the Father has for us. This is a tremendous debt I cannot repay.

By entering the birthing canal of Christ, however, I'm en route to saying thank you.

I know that I'm on the right road that leads to eternal life.

Are you?

 bridge over
troubled waters...

---

*"And which of you
by being anxious
can add
a single cubit
to his life's span?"*

Matthew 6:27

CHAPTER FOURTEEN

Rising out of the waters of Lake Huron and Lake Michigan lies a priceless archway. This massive thesis joins together the upper peninsula and the lower half of Michigan. A structure know as The Mackinac Bridge. A five-mile framework spanning the blue waters below. A magnificent composition.

As a young child, I encountered this arrangement of concrete. Every Labor Day weekend, there's a tradition to open up this bridge to walkers. The two northbound lanes are closed off to traffic and are used for this merry little parade. The two southbound lanes then become single lanes to be used for the automotive traffic.

I remember the afternoon quite well. It was a mild day. A day I will never forget.

There was so much to see. So much to do. The waters stretched into the horizon and disappeared over it's cliff. Huge ships journeyed the depths below. Birds soared the never- ending skies. Planes traveled the distant blue yonder. We sang. We laughed. We conversed. We basked in the afternoon sun. It was delightful.

The halfway point, however, was the turning point. Everything took on a new meaning. The anticipation I had of marching across this bridge overshadowed the bathroom break that I should have taken before our departure.

I can still recall asking my father, "when will we be there?"

This line finds much ridicule on our family vacations but I wasn't laughing on this one. This was for real. My bladder was crying from the inside and greatly affecting my outside. As you know, brothers and sisters don't usually supply sympathy during this type of crisis but usually aid the forbidden source in hopes of an eruption.

"Two and half miles to go," my father said.

That is a long way to go when you are in imminent need of a bathroom but it is an endless nightmare when you are surrounded by water.

Every step was painful. Every stride was torture. The only thing I wanted more than anything else was to rid myself of the tremendous burden raging within my bladder.

The truth of this story is we let it happen in our own lives. We start down a particular passageway and get sidetracked with discouragement, pain and uncomfortable circumstances. What begins as a pleasant little step somehow turns into a sprint toward the finish line.

Okay, you're right. It's understandable to be oblivious of the surroundings to be in a hurry during such a normal human function.

Is it right, however, to be spiritually impatient risking the well-being of others for our own spiritual gain? We can't even stop and see the needs of others because of our own compassionate blindness. Is doing the Holy-hustle worth personal treasure?

Why are we in such a hurry to get to our destinations? Always rushing toward the end product. Too often we live life like a predator after it's prey or like the hunter stalking the hunted.

There is so much along the way we miss when our entire focus is just getting the job done. Some of the best memories happen while we journey up the walk and not necessarily upon arriving at the front door.

"And which of you by being anxious can add a single cubit to his life's span?" (Matthew 6:27)

Do you know what the word "anxious" really means?

It means to be troubled, worried. Eagerly desiring. To choke. To cause distress.

Webster painted a pretty good picture. It's simply impossible to smell the surrounding vegetation when we're standing knee-deep in manure.

Spiritual burnout happens when we develop this impatient mindset. We can't allow the devil's meager schemes to overshadow the Lord's enormous victories simply because the picture isn't unfolding fast enough.

Let's look at the basics.

It's not the trophies we brag about. It's the road we walked achieving them. It's not the medals we're displaying. It's those hurdles we crossed to receive them.

Imagine if life was always lived with the finished product in hand. No need to play the game. Just simply flip a coin and the winner takes all. Pretty boring. No exciting plays to recall. No hall of fame moments to enjoy. Just a winner. Just a loser.

What makes the victory so rewarding are the highlights that we recite following the game. Those unforgettable plays we recount in wild conversation. Those earth-shattering events that make the newspaper headlines. It is the journey and not the end result we choose to fondly remember.

Give it some thought.

What makes the lounge chair so comfortable? A hard day's work of stressful labor.

What makes ice tea so refreshing? The hours spent under the hot rays of the sun.

Keep in mind it is the intense heat that makes air conditioning so rejuvenating. It's those sub-zero temperatures that makes the cozy blanket so inviting.

We all know that you can't enjoy a book if you always read the last chapter first.

Please don't get me wrong. I can't wait to be home with my Father in Heaven. It's precisely this thought, however, that makes each day a precious gift.

So the next time you're flying down the intestates and highways of your life attempting to break those records of getting from here to there, don't miss the wonderful opportunity of being with family and friends. Relish the stunning landscapes. Ponder the Holiness of Christ.

There are plenty of rest areas along the way if your bridge is holding troubled waters.

Up! Up! and away with your beautiful balloons

*"Come to Me,
all who
are weary and heavy-laden,
and I
will give you rest."*

Matthew 11:28

CHAPTER FIFTEEN

The balloons traveled with him wherever he went. They would float just a few feet above his head. He loved watching them. Even at night the balloons would drift above his head while he slept.

Everyone who knew the balloon man was accustomed to seeing the balloons. Those who worked by his side didn't mind them either. They brightened their lives as well.

One day the man went to the county fair. He blended into the atmosphere of rides, lights and noises. There were some who tried to buy his balloons, thinking he was a vendor, but he would not sell a single one.

He visited many exhibits. At one booth he filled out a slip of paper and put it into a box. It was a drawing for a free ocean cruise. He certainly didn't plan on winning but it never hurt to try.

Two weeks later, to his surprise, the telegram arrived. He had won! He was so excited. The thought of traveling the mighty ocean waters unparalleled any previous adventure he had encountered.

Immediately, he began to pack. He was ready days before the ship's departure.

On the morning of the big day he called a taxi to drive him to the boating docks. Some of the wealth of his balloons had to travel outside the window. Slowly they roved through the city streets making their way toward the harbor.

Upon his arrival he quickly unloaded his luggage and boarded the ship. The balloon man was welcomed by officials who had planned his trip. They even had one of the ship's crew take his belongings to his cabin while he remained on deck to enjoy the festivities.

The ship was crowded.

There was confetti flying, horns blaring, streamers soaring and colorful balloons everywhere. He felt right at home.

Finally the voyage commenced.

The ocean air was refreshing. The south sea breeze was invigorating.

All of the morning excitement and afternoon activities made him very hungry. One of the stewards told the balloon man the evening meal would soon be tendered. A welcome relief.

The dinner bell rang. The balloon man merged toward the dining room. The aroma was enticing. The flavor was engaging.

The door, however, wasn't large enough for the man and his balloons. The balloon man would have to unburden a few of his balloons but he refused the suggestion. The thought was appalling.

He had seen some crackers and cheese on the upper deck previously and decided to settle with their fill. It wasn't the finest meal he'd ever eaten but it was adequate.

The sunset on the ocean was awesome. The gleam cast a breathtaking sight. Gulls danced in the evening shadows. The waves resolved into soft foam.

He strolled the deck.

The evening air began to chill. The balloon man grew tired. The excitement of the day had simply worn him out.

He asked one of ship's crew members to show him his quarters. The man accompanied him down a corridor and opened the door to his cabin.

It was luxurious. They had given him one the finest rooms on the ship. He could see the interior was of vintage decor.

The bed was very inviting.

Unfortunately the door wasn't big enough for the man and his balloons to enter the vogue surroundings. He tried but his efforts failed.

Back on deck he found some blankets and a deck chair. He tied the balloons securely around his wrist and collapsed into a deep sleep.

The next morning arrived much too quickly. The balloon man was still very tired. The chair did not renew an once of his vigor.

Throughout the day the balloon man ate cheese and crackers and lounged and mulled around in complete exhaustion. Once again he returned to the deck chair for slumber.

The next morning the balloon man received an engraved invitation from the ship's captain. He had been invited to sit at the captain's table and enjoy the specialty of the world-famous chef prepared especially for him.

All day he watched as the crew made preparations for the evening banquet to be held in his honor. The anticipation was overwhelming. The suspense was joyful.

At eight o'clock the dinner bell rang. Passengers began to file into the dining hall. The balloon man observed them as they prepared for the evening's soiree.

He stood at the end of the passageway for quite some time. He could hear the murmur of voices, the sound of silverware rattling and the clinking of glasses as the gala unfolded.

Finally, he walked to the back of the ship in disappointment.

The mumbling of the dinner guests lingered in the background while loneliness was ever so present in the foreground.

He reached deeply into his pocket and pulled out his engraved invitation. He recalled the special place reserved for him at the captain's table.

He looked at the balloons and then at his invitation. Back and forth he deliberated his circumstance. From balloons to invitation he pondered his dilemma. The decision was of highest magnitude.

Slowly he began to uncurl his fingers. His muscles ached as he loosened his grip. He could feel the string as it slowly evaded his grasp.

One by one the balloons began to drift away. He watched them as they slowly disappeared into the night.

He turned and began to walk down the passageway. A weight seemed to be lifted with every step.

He opened the door and stepped into the banquet hall.

That night as a guest at the captain's table, the once known balloon man enjoyed the finest meal and best companionship he had ever known.

You too have been invited to sit at the Captain's table. Your name has been engraved upon the invitation. A chair has been reserved in your honor. You may need to lose some baggage to enter the mighty throne room. You might have to let go of worldly balloons to find yourself present at the Captain's table.

The end, however, definitely outweighs your means.

Let go!

"Come to Me, all who are weary and heavy-laden, and I will give you rest. Take My yoke upon you, and learn from Me, for I am gentle and humble in heart; and you shall find rest for your souls." (Matthew 11:28,29)

Up! Up! and Away with your beautiful balloons!

oes anyone care?

"For God so love the world, that He gave His only begotten Son, that whoever believe in Him should not perish, but have eternal life."

John 3:16

CHAPTER SIXTEEN

As you read this story, give careful thought to the entire portrayal. Consider what is taking place. Ponder the entire meaning.

I abid you adieu until it's conclusion.

The son loved his father. The father loved his son. They both proudly displayed their affections.

The old man labored hard for his son. His job was neither luxurious nor glorious. He was paid a small wage. He was content, however, for it was a job.

The old man worked at a railway station. His job was to lower and raise the drawbridge.

Daily, trains would make their way across the bridge while boats would trek the river carrying imported produce and cargo.

The boy desperately wanted his father to take him to work. The old man refused because of the dangerous surroundings. The boy persisted. Day in and out he begged his father.

Like most fathers who look into their child's beaming eyes, he couldn't resist. At last, he gave in.

The boy couldn't sleep the entire night. He was not going to miss this once-in-a-lifetime opportunity.

When the old man awoke, he was startled. Not even two feet from his face stood a bright-eyed, grinning boy. With the constant pulling on his arm and an immature voice beckoning, the two of them marched off to work.

The day was filled with an assortment of gadgetry. The old man showed his son countless contraptions.

The boy was overwhelmed by the gigantic boats. Thrilled by the trains. This was the largest toy box a child could ever imagine. Only his dreams had treated him with such wonderful treasures.

Mid-afternoon came too suddenly. The old man had lost track of time. He glanced at his watch and realized that the four o'clock train would be making its way back to the surrounding villages. Hundreds of people would be returning to their homes aboard the liner. He knew he needed to lower the bridge immediately. He grabbed his boy's hand and quickly raced across the yard to his work place.

It was an open two-story building that housed the gears that worked the drawbridge. An old wooden ladder about twelve feet high scaled the wall of the building. A plank connected the ladder to a platform on the opposite wall. The gear wheels laid directly below the plank. From this platform, the bridge was raised and lowered.

Once they were inside, the old man led the young lad to the ladder and hastily made their ascent. He followed his son up the ladder. At the top of the ladder the old man impatiently cut in front of his son and began to cross the unrailed walkway. Not thinking the young lad would follow, the old man pushed the lever forward, engaging the tons of metal that made up the iron wheels.

The ancient timbers of the building began to shake. The boy tried to steady his feet and keep his balance but tumbled into the vicious teeth below.

The boy cried out in agony.

The old man quickly pulled back the lever bringing the gears to a halt.

Panic etched into the father's wrinkled form. An eerie sensation graced his tired body.

His son screamed in pain. His blood was pooling on the concrete below.

The father began to tremble. His thoughts began racing as he tried to formulate a plan to free his son. His brow began to bead with sweat.

The boy bellowed in anguish.

The father's callused hands began to shake. Tears began to develop in the old man's eyes.

"I must keep my composure," he thought to himself.

He knew the afternoon train would emerge from around the bend carrying hundreds of people returning to their nearby villages.

"The bridge must be completely lowered," he thought to himself, "or all of the passengers would be lost."

Standing between their life and death was his only son.

The old man grieved for his son, his mind racing back and forth between his only two alternatives: his precious son's life or a train filled with unknowing people.

The boy shrieked in torment.

There was no time to descend the ladder. No time to formulate a plan. Not a second remained for a rescue. The choice he must make was becoming painfully clear. Time was of the essence.

A decision was reached.

Far from the desires of his heart, the old man placed his left hand over his eyes and his right hand on the controls. He prayed earnestly. With his head tilted back, he cried a plea of mercy and then pushed the lever forward.

His son's voice was no longer heard.

The heavy machinery jarred a little as the body passed through it's rotation.

Then all was silent. The stillness was frightening. Only the wind softly whispered.

The old man stood there as time momentarily stopped. His worst nightmare had just come true.

Suddenly, a booming train whistle rang out from around the bend. The old man turned and looked up the distant tracks. From around the corner loomed the afternoon train. It was moving across the tracks with ease and stability. The roar of the engine echoed off the hillside and the steam filled the sunlit sky. One by one the train cars began to pass in front of the railway station.

Scene after scene passed before the father's eyes. Window after window displayed it's own motion picture.

A young lad was sitting eagerly in front of a bowl of ice cream getting ready to thrust his spoon into it's pleasure.

A conductor was counting his tickets.

A businessman sat intently before an opened briefcase, deliberating his day's work.

A girl and a young man were affectionately embracing one another.

Person after person and situation after situation kept passing before the eyes of the old man.

The old man grew angry. He began to call out to the train and it's passengers.

"Does anyone care? Does anyone care? I just gave my only son for you."

His fist clenched and his arms raised.

"Does anyone care?"

His voice tried to resound above the thrust of the train engine.

"Does anyone care?" he softly spoke.

"Does anyone care?" he quietly whispered.

He began to weep.

The train passed into history. The rattling of the tracks grew quiet.

Tears poured from the old man's eyes as he slowly made his way to the remains of his only son. He knelt beside his mangled and unrecognizable form.

He whispered, "I love you."

While searching the ceiling rafters the endless question plagued his shattered mind, "Does anyone care?"

What more is there to say?

This story is not new. We've all heard about the accounts of Jesus Christ. We've seen the illustrations of His death in pictures, magazines and books. People wear the symbol around their necks. Churches present the cruxification atop their steeples. Conversations carry the message. It spans the entire globe.

It's hard for you and I to comprehend a father who would

sacrifice his only son for a life he didn't know. However, this story is not fiction.

Our Heavenly Father willingly shed the innocent blood of His Son for you and I. It wasn't a choice made in lieu of circumstance but a decision that was ordained before the Child's birth. Jesus Christ was marching toward the cross well before His manger scene in Bethlehem. He was on His way to the cross prior to the conception.

It was inevitable.

This blood was yielded in love. God saw our struggle with sin and became sin for us, to free us from death's grip. There was no choice to be made. He wasn't delayed by indecision. The questions were overruled by His affirmation. It was the only way for you and I to share eternity with our Heavenly Father.

He cared.

Jesus Christ completely covered everything with His precious blood. He envisioned our lives as the absolute best and set in motion the entire menu that we would need to order from.

You don't have to pick and chose. Every answer is simply, "all the above."

So are you ready to begin this incredible journey? Has the hodgepodge completely caught up with you? Is it time to dream new dreams? Is this your opportunity to again have a life with vision, meaning and purpose?

Unmarked territories are just over the horizon. The engine is ready. Steam is pouring from its stack. Plenty of coal has been reserved for the trip. The conductor is standing at the edge of the tracks just waiting for you to hand him your ticket and step aboard this train.

It's simple. The passport is free.

Just pray this prayer:

"Jesus. I've lost myself to the daily demands of this world. Forgive me for my sin. Replace my human wants and desires with your righteous will. I am no longer my own. I am Your child.

Rekindle my long lost dreams. Restore my forgotten passions. I will no longer live to survive but forever will be be revived by the renewal of the Holy Spirit.

Amen."

Open your eyes. Look around. The scenery is a novel. Your life is just about to begin. A brand new person is about to come alive.

Do you remember those books of dreams that you once had placed upon the forgotten shelf of humanity?

Reach up and take one down. Go ahead, dust off it's cover. Blow away those cobwebs of discouragement. Start exploring it's pages one more time. Things are totally different. The new author is unbeaten. He's been patiently waiting for an opportunity like this. He can't wait to put His pen to the paper.

So take hold of the vintage manuscript. Find a nice shade tree. Sit beneath it's limbs and enjoy. This life will once again be filled with a fresh excitement and a unprecedented meaning.

You are going to love the story line! The author had you in mind when he wrote it.

Happy reading.